Published by Beverly's Children's Books
Illustrated by Bex Sutton

Copyright @ 2024 by Beverly King
beverlyschildrensbooks@gmail.com

ACROSS:

2. WHAT DO CATS HAVE THAT KEEP THEM WARM?

3. A CAT WITHOUT A HOME

4. KEEPING AN ANIMAL IS CALLED A...

DOWN:

1. "_____ FINDS A HOME"

2. SOMETHING CATS LOVE TO EAT

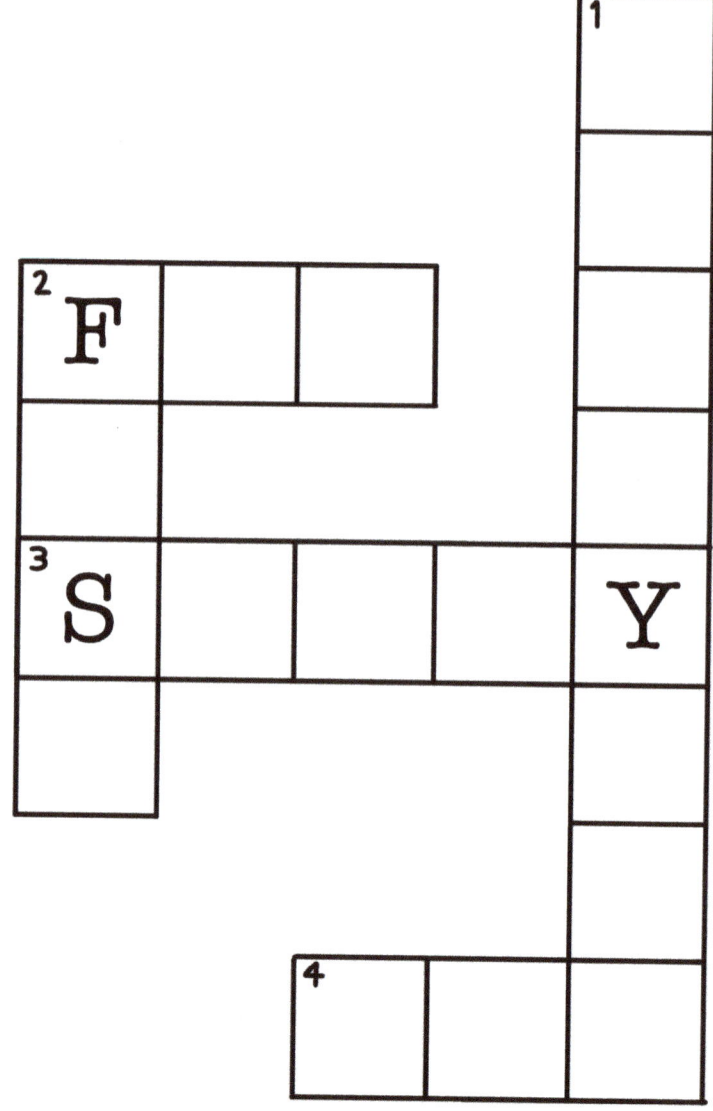

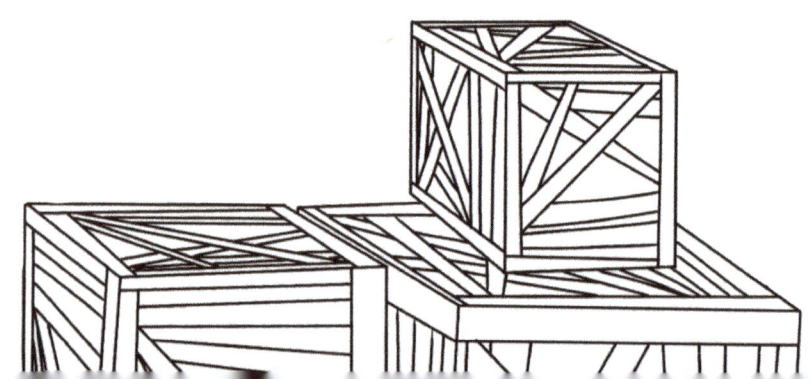

Lead Millie through the maze to the bowl of food!

Connect the dots!

Can you spot all the hidden insects?

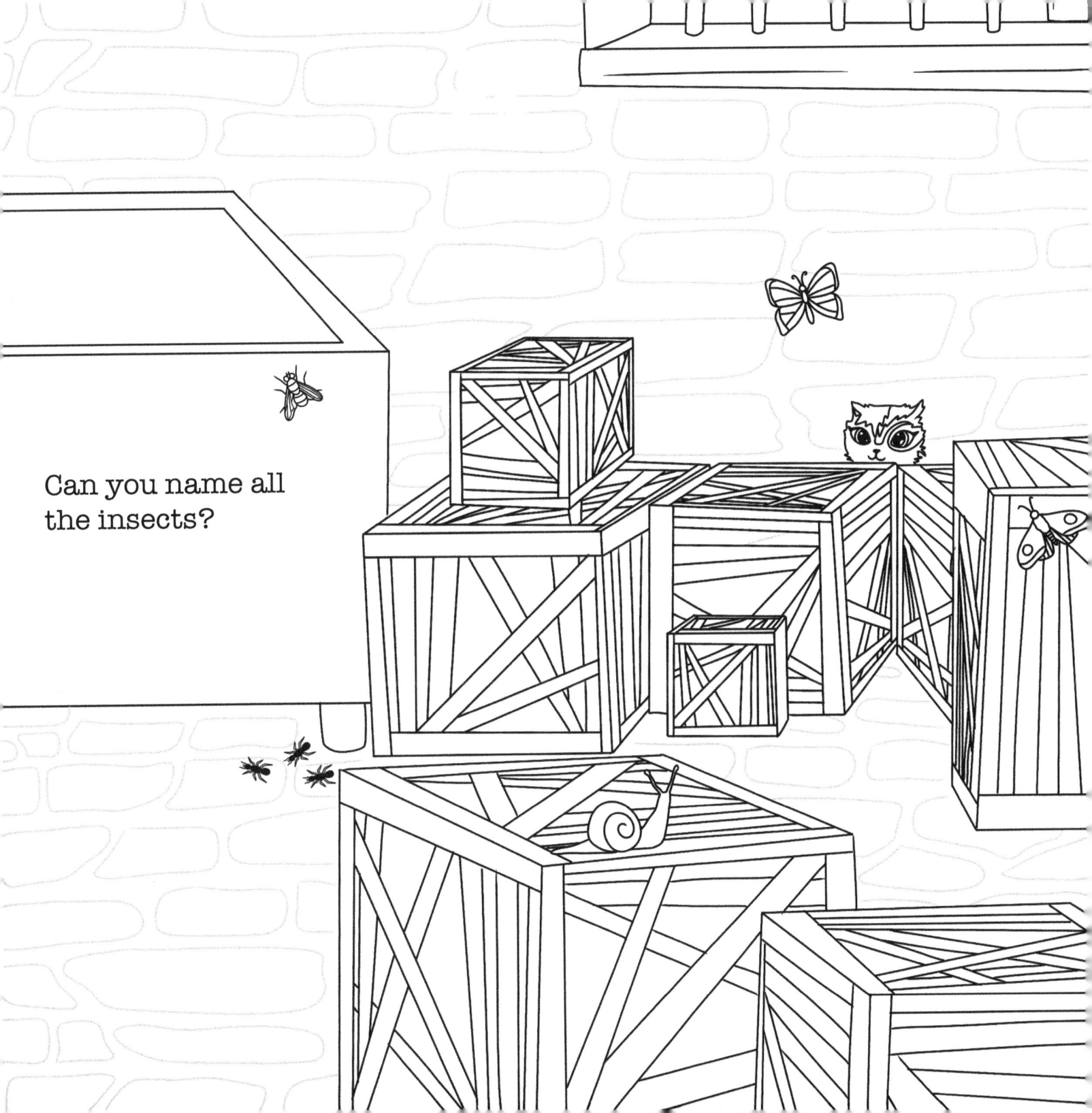

Can you name all
the insects?

END

START

Can you draw a new cat friend for Millie?

Grid 1:

	+	9	+		24
+	■		+	■	+
	+		+	4	8
+	■		+	■	+
	+		+		13
16		12		17	

Grid 2:

6	+		+		21
+	■	+	■	+	
5	+		+		8
+	■	+	■	+	
	+		+		16
20		11		14	

```
S F A P Y B C C P Y
F T X Z I A T W I W
H K R R E S A L N S
J H N I H O M U T F
F V N A N L S A A N
V R B T Y G E Y C H
B H X Y B R P J O K
A T C E T X M B L T
L T L F E A T H E R
L L X Y R I B B O N
```

BALL
BELL
CATNIP
FEATHER
LASER
RIBBON
STRING
TOYS
TREATS

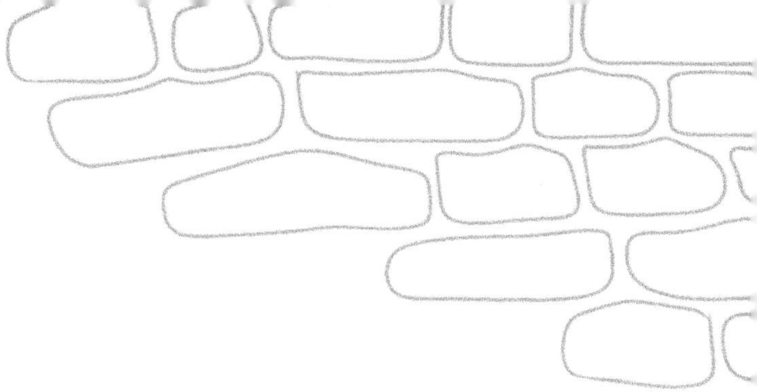

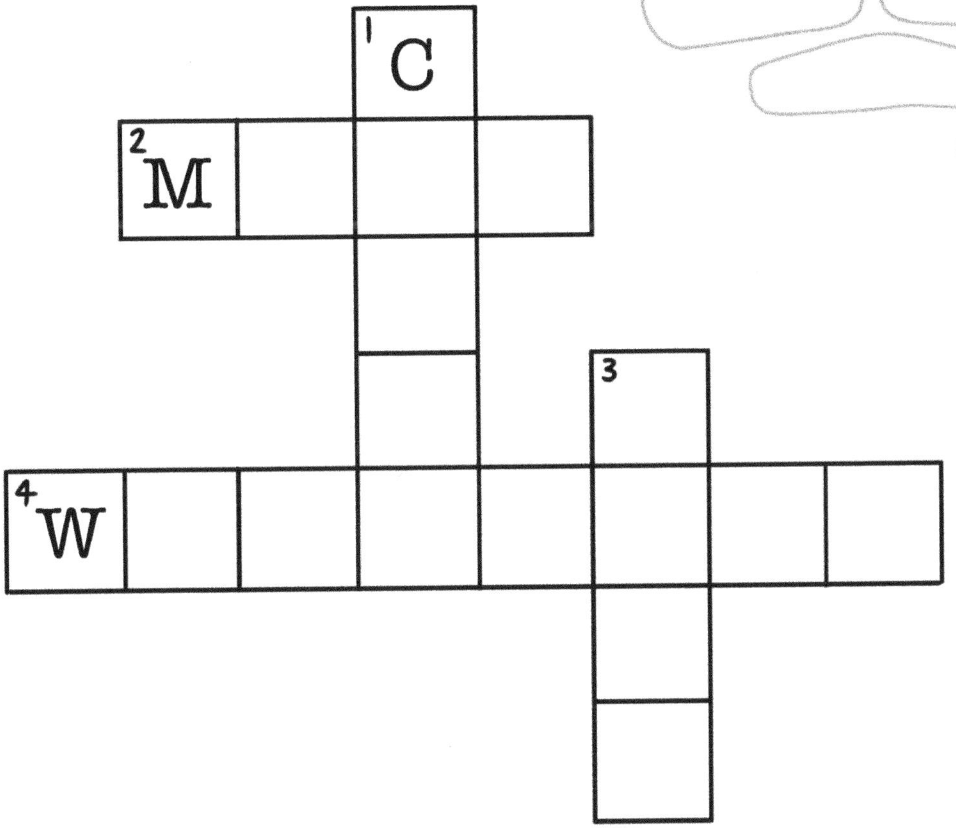

ACROSS

2. WHAT DO KITTENS DRINK?

4. FEATURES ON A CATS FACE

DOWN

1. THESE ARE VERY SHARP

3. THE SOUND A CAT MAKES

Copy the pictue of Millie below on the next page by filling in the empty squares.

Spot the difference!

Can you find all the hidden flowers?

```
E C R S R R U R W D
Y M T T E A G M J M
N E O S T T W X M Z
V X C H L D R Q T U
T U S H E A L T H Y
E K P C H D P E Q R
E G O P S T B O Z H
E U T Y F Z H P Y A
T A C Y E L L A N E
F Y J O D T S X A K
```

ALLEYCAT
HEALTHY
HOME
RESCUE
SHELTER
VETS

Can you draw a picture of Millie playing with a ball of string?

ACROSS:

3. NOT FLUFFY, BUT
_____.

4. A CATS SHARP
NAILS

DOWN:

1. WHEN A CAT
PURRS IT MEANS
THEY ARE...

2. A TYPE OF FISH

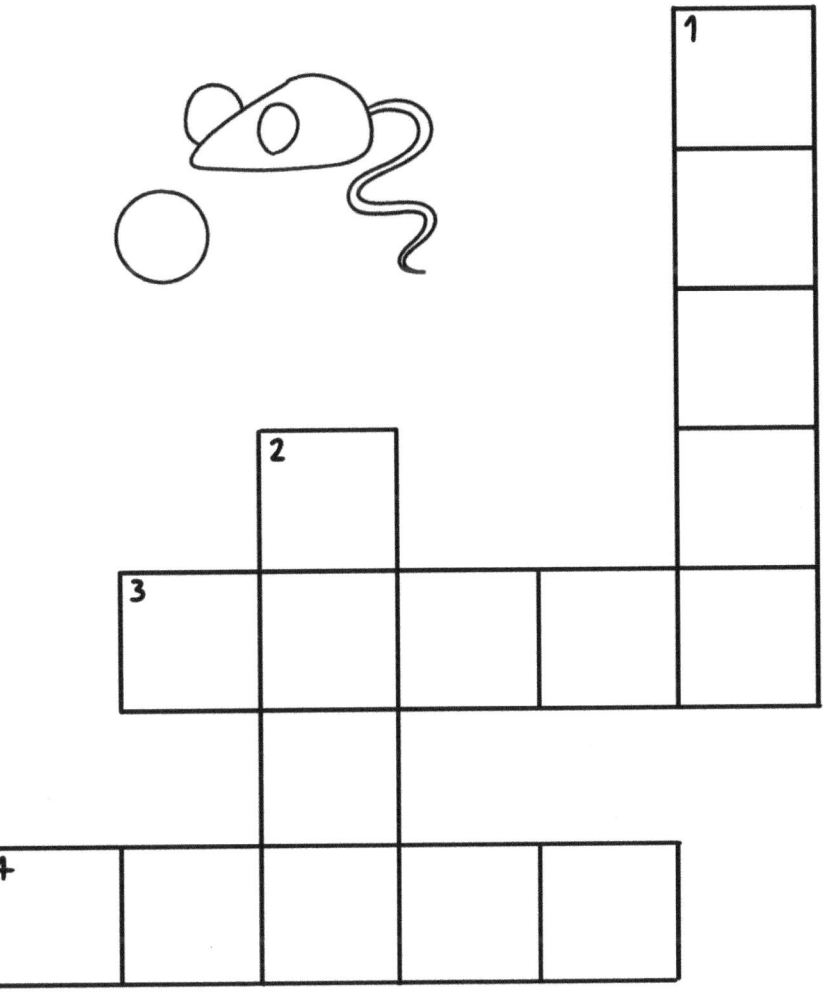

```
K C S N O U D S Y F
Y A T X O F T P T E
K L S R N R A A P L
S I U W A V B W E I
U C T Y A B G D S N
H O I T Y L M G G E
F Y C S E Q C Y M C
Y E L L A N C A T I
W H I S K E R S G X
S W O E M X O Y H T
```

ALLEY
CALICO
CAT
CLAWS
FELINE
KITTEN
MEOW
PAWS
STRAY
TABBY
WHISKERS

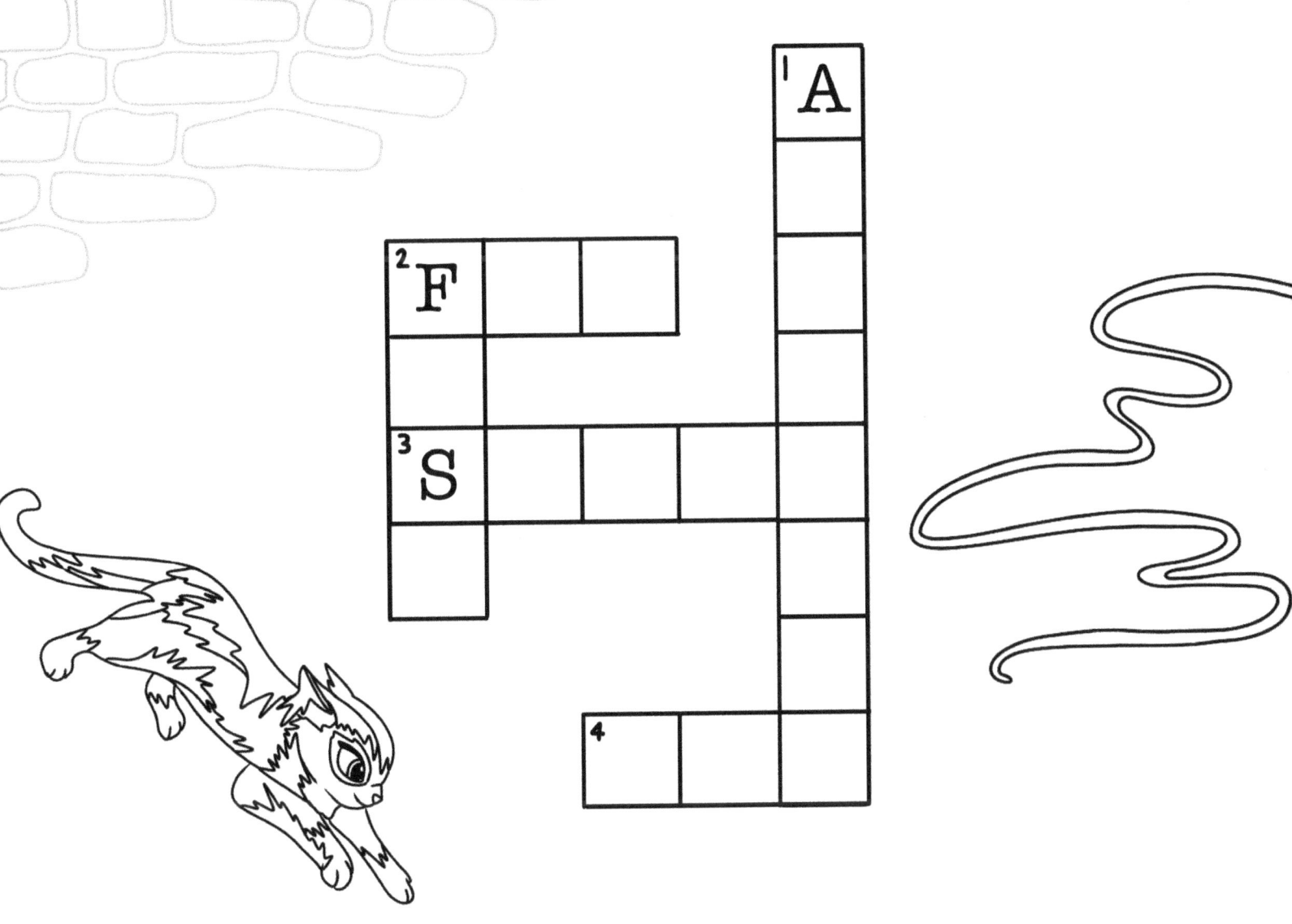

ACROSS

2. WHAT DO CATS HAVE THAT KEEP THEM WARM?

3. A CAT WITHOUT A HOME

4. KEEPING AN ANIMAL IS CALLED A ___.

DOWN

1. THE TITLE OF THIS BOOK

2. SOMETHING CATS LOVE TO EAT

Can you draw a picture of other animals that Millie may have
seen at the vets?

Right grid row sums: 13, 13, 19
Right grid column sums: 15, 17, 13

Left grid row sums: 15, 20, 10
Left grid column sums: 11, 24, 10

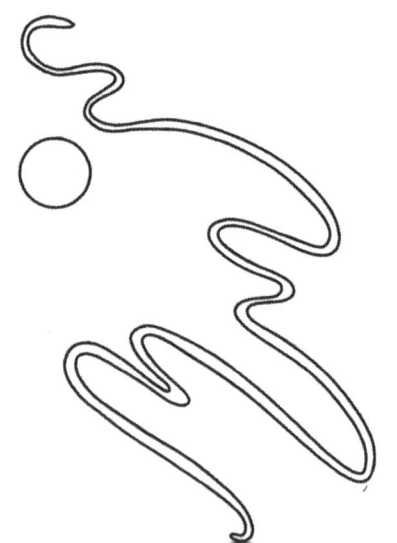

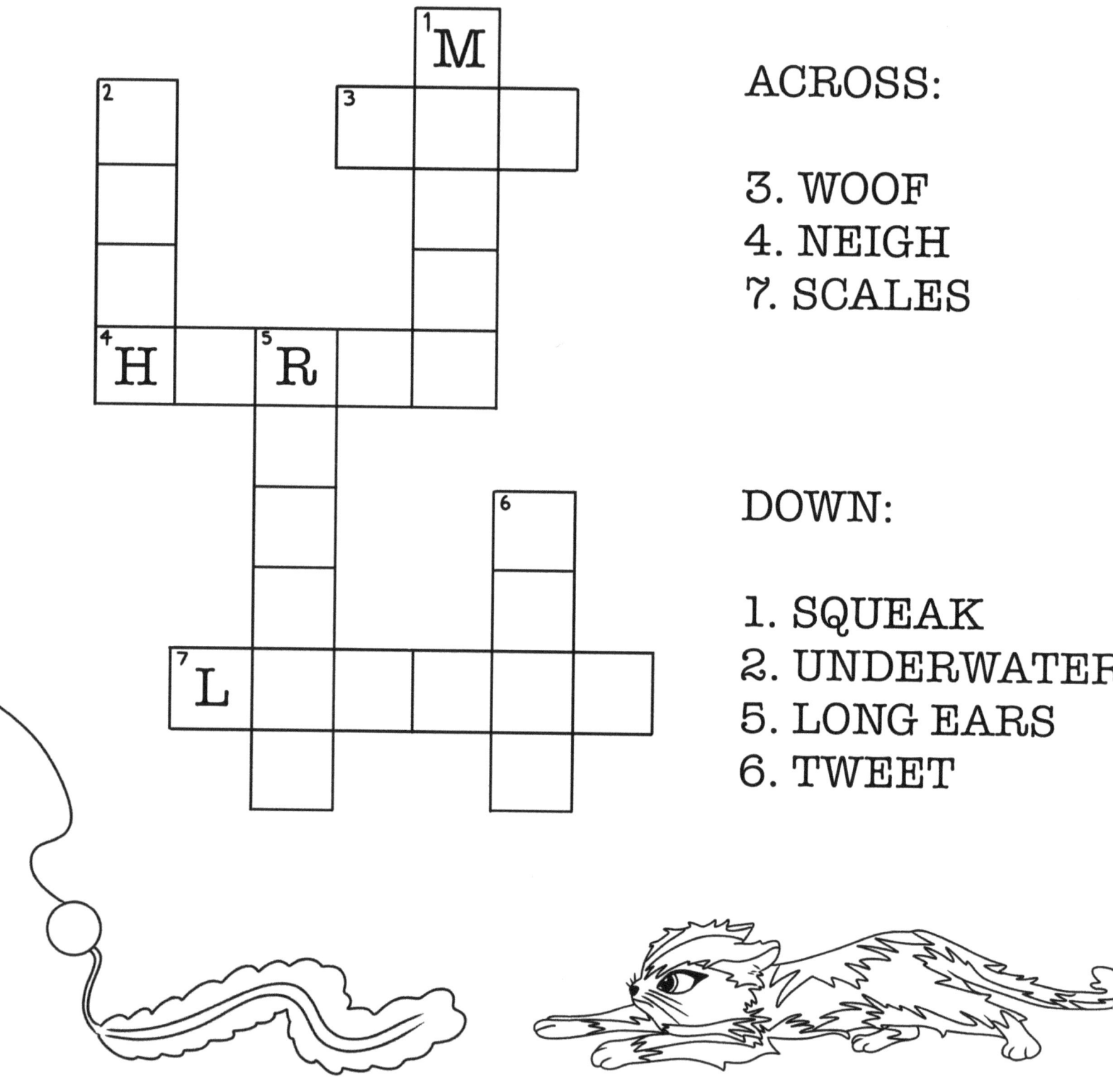

ACROSS:

3. WOOF
4. NEIGH
7. SCALES

DOWN:

1. SQUEAK
2. UNDERWATER
5. LONG EARS
6. TWEET

How many hidden birds
are in the picture?

LITTER BOX

Connect
the dots!

```
M J R A Q B R E T Q
H T P O D A M U O I
C U B O L R Q I W R
T Q A L U G V P L G
A P O C D N K G O C
R C B E L L C D O I
C Q F Z A Q N E G V
S E Q X H Y S N G B
O Z V H Y Z G W S D
G B B Z X X I P Q B
```

ADOPT   COLLAR

BELL   POUNCE

CLIMB   SCRATCH

LITTER BOX

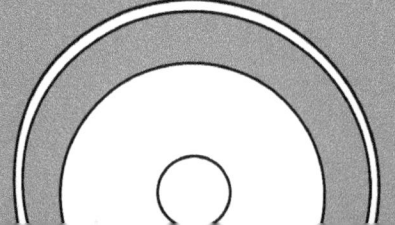

Draw your own cat photo:

Draw a picture of you cuddling Millie

Left grid

	+	1	+	4	**11**
+	■	+	■	+	
	+		+		**18**
+	■	+	■	+	
	+		+		**16**
11		**15**		**19**	

Right grid

	+		+		**17**
+	■	+	■	+	
4	+	5	+		**15**
+	■	+	■	+	
	+		+		**13**
14		**14**		**17**	

Can you find all the hidden fruit? _____

LITTER BOX

ACROSS

2. A BABY CAT

3. WHAT ARE CATS HANDS AND FEET CALLED?

DOWN

1. WHEN A CAT IS SCARED, THEY ____.

3. WHAT IS MILLIE?

Spot the difference!

Copy this pictue of Millie and Maxine on the next page by filling in the empty squares.

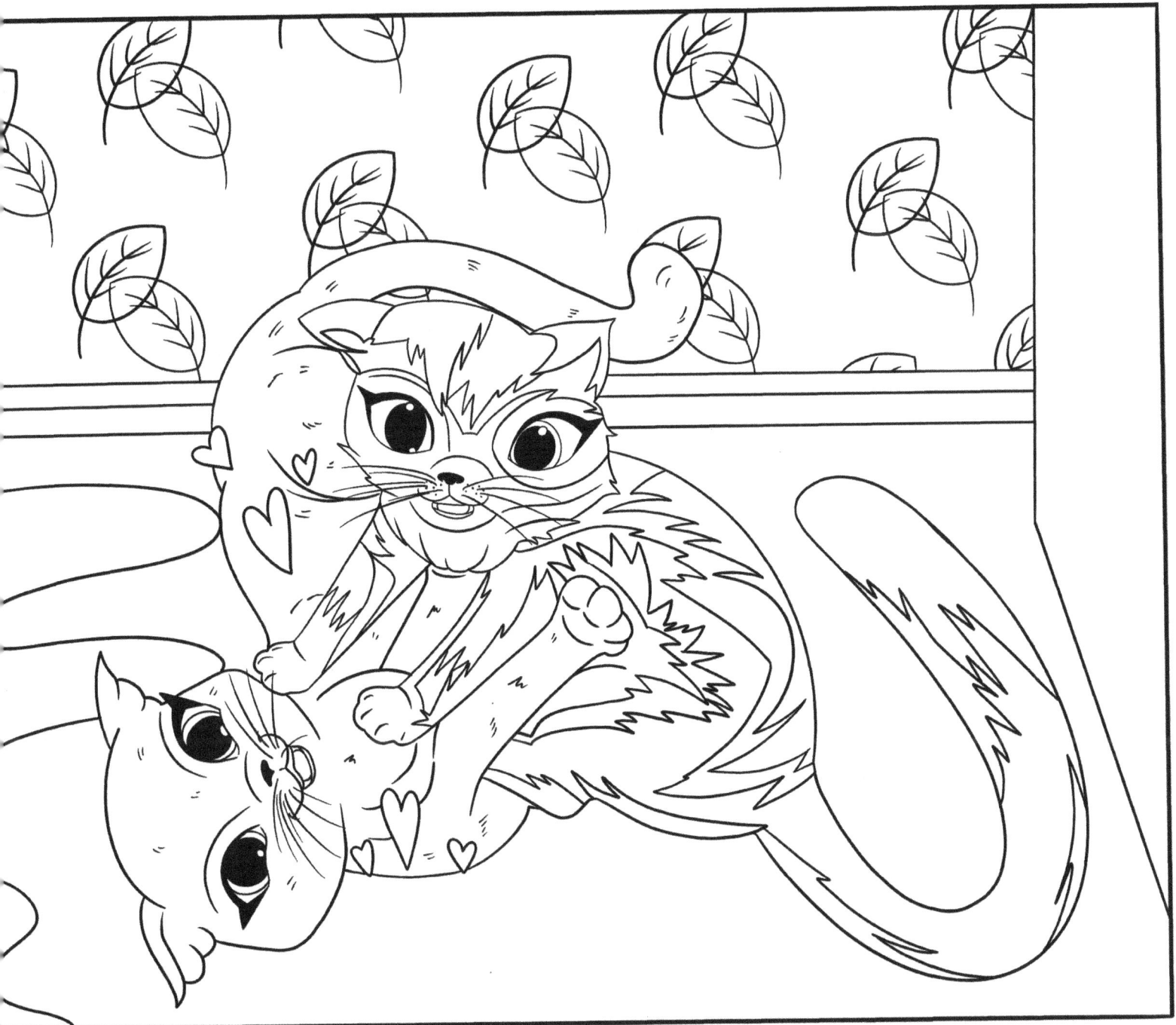

END

START

Draw a picture of Lilly

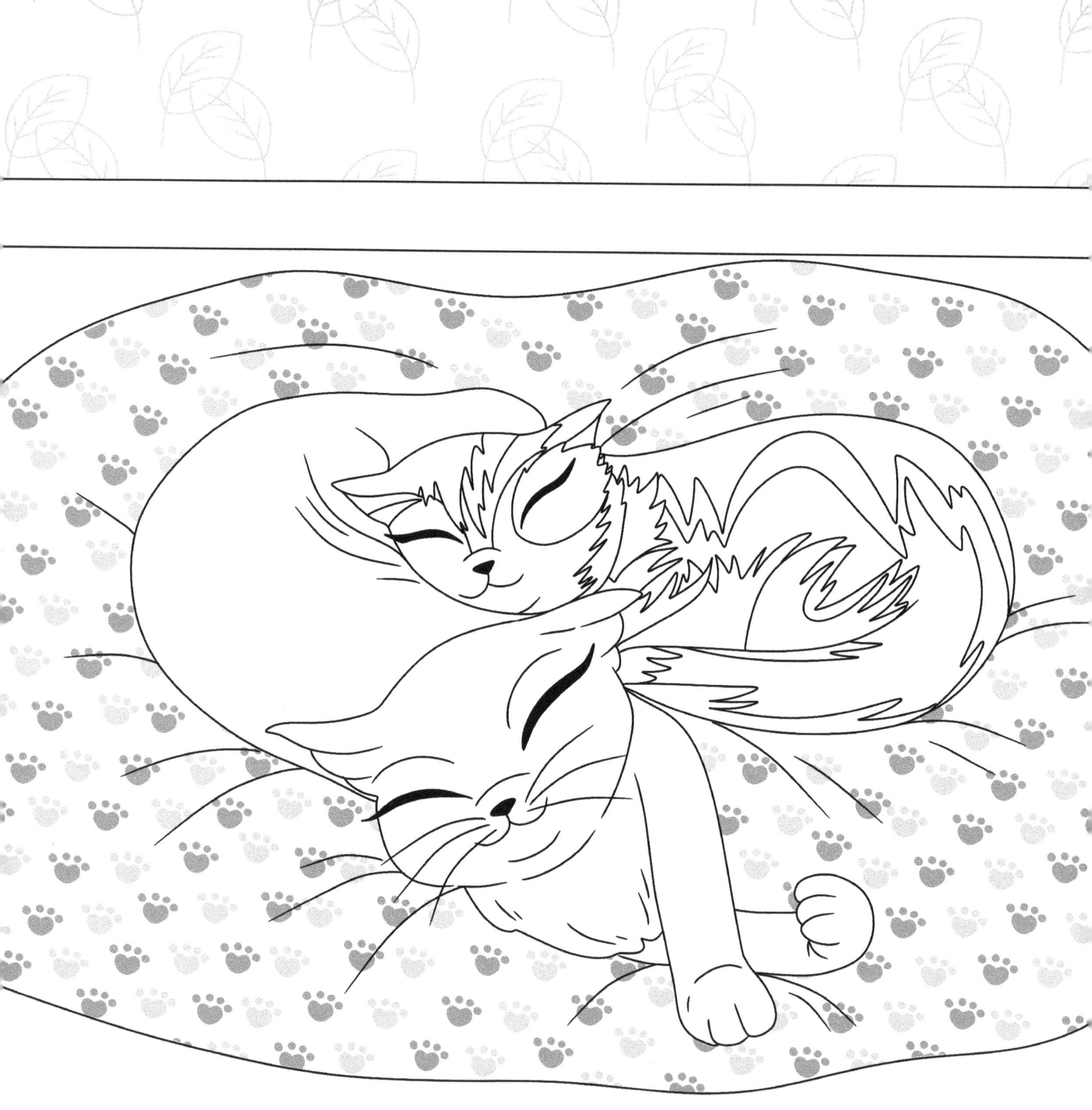

```
U K S K T A P K F G
U I K P V S M D I N
Y T N T B V S W V I
F T A N I M A L P R
I E T Z A X E E E R
J N L I O B T T X U
S A K I K O U R D P
P X Z O N C L O V E
U I L D V E T A C V
S H N Y T H B U A U
```

ANIMAL	FELINE	LOVE
CAT	KITTEN	PET
CUTE	KITTY	PURRING

ACROSS

2. CATS HAVE A VERY ROUGH _____.

3. A CATS BATHROOM

DOWN

1. WHAT CATS DO WITH THEIR PAWS WHEN THEY ARE COMFY

4. A BIG STRIPEY CAT

Copy this pictue of Bob, Lilly and Millie on the next page by filling in the empty squares.

What are Lilly and Milly dreaming of?

END

START

ACROSS

2. When a cat seeks a quiet or safe place, often under a bed or in a box.

5. What cats love to do on trees or furniture.

6. The process of taking in a cat to become part of your family.

7. A cat that doesn't have a home and roams the streets.

DOWN

1. A breed of cat with long, fluffy fur.

3. A small box where a cat goes to the bathroom indoors.

4. A breed of cat known for its sleek body and blue eyes.

Puzzle 1:

	−	5	+		2
+	■	+	■	+	
	+		+	9	17
−	■	−	■	+	
	+		+		16
5		4		20	

Puzzle 2:

	+		−	3	8
−	■	+	■	−	
5	+		+		13
−	■	−	■	+	
	−		+		0
1		1		9	

Draw a picture of a cat in your house

Can you spot all the cats?

How many balls are in the picture?

LITTER BOX

START

END

START

END

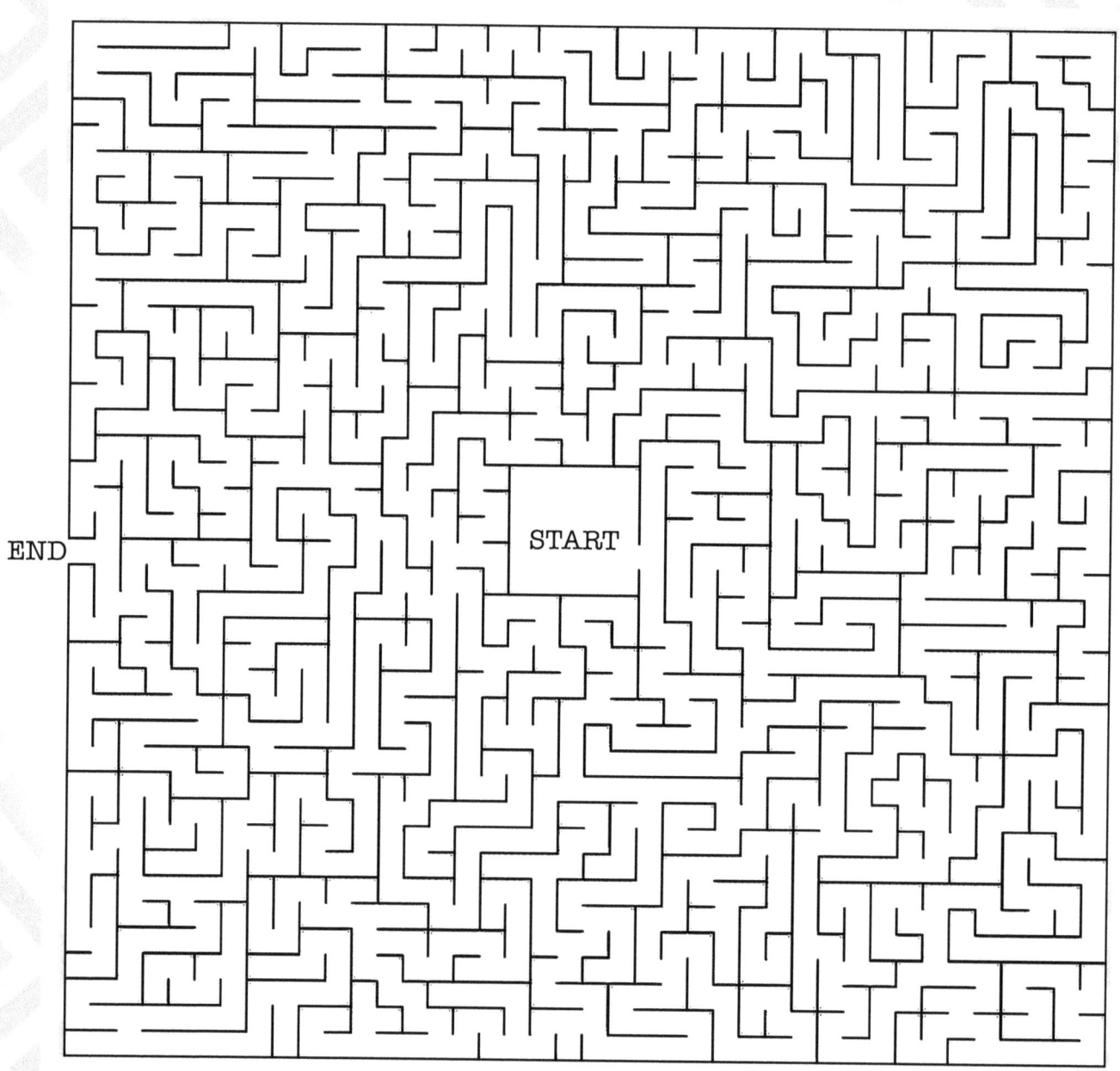

Draw a picture of kittens playing with each other

We hope you've enjoyed this Activity Book!
You can find more of Beverly King children's
books on Amazon.